GENERAL DIRECTIONS

THE CANVAS GRID

All of these projects were worked on plastic canvas sheets, with seven stitches to the inch, called 7-mesh plastic canvas. We have used regular weight canvas, available in sheets measuring 10½" x 13½", and extra-stiff and extra-soft, available in sheets measuring 12" x 18". Extra-stiff canvas provides an especially firm stitching surface and can be used for any section of a project that does not need to be bent or shaped. Extra-soft canvas is appropriate for pieces that do need to be bent or shaped.

THE PATTERN CHARTS AND EQUIPMENT

There is a pattern chart for most stitched pieces. However, some square or rectangular pieces may not be charted; follow the instructions noted in the individual project. The color keys near the charts indicate the color and type of stitch to use.

You will need a size 16 or 18 tapestry needle for stitching, a grease pencil or felt pen to mark the pattern shape on the canvas, and strong scissors and a sharp craft knife to cut the canvas.

THE YARN

Any yarn that covers the canvas can be used with plastic canvas. You may use one strand worsted weight yarn, nylon needlecraft yarn, rug yarn or craft yarn. If you prefer, you may use two strands of needlepoint tapestry wool or three strands of Persian-type yarn. When working with double or triple strands, remember to increase the yarn amounts accordingly. When working with most yarn, use a 36" length for stitching; use an 18" length if yarn tends to fray.

CUTTING THE CANVAS

All of our patterns are measured by bars, not holes. Mark the outline of each piece on the plastic canvas and cut them (**Fig 1**), using scissors or craft knife for small areas. Trim any plastic nubs and cut corners on the diagonal (**Fig 2**); be careful not to cut so close that the corner is weakened.

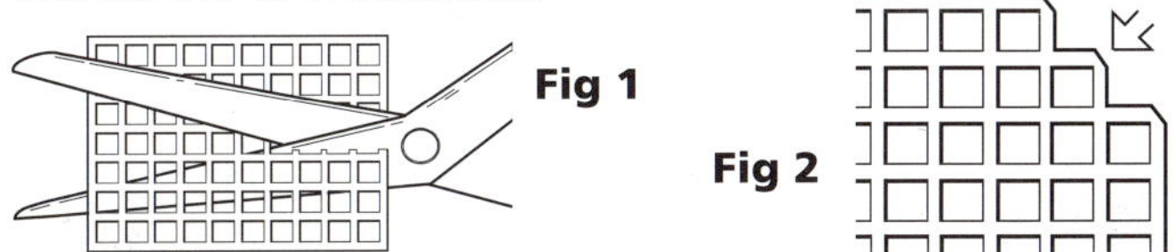

BEGINNING AND ENDING

Do not tie a knot to begin stitching with a new strand. Hold an inch of the end in place and work the first few stitches over the end (**Fig 3**). You may also anchor the end by running it through a few stitches of an adjacent stitched area. End strand by running it through the back of a stitched area and trim it closely.

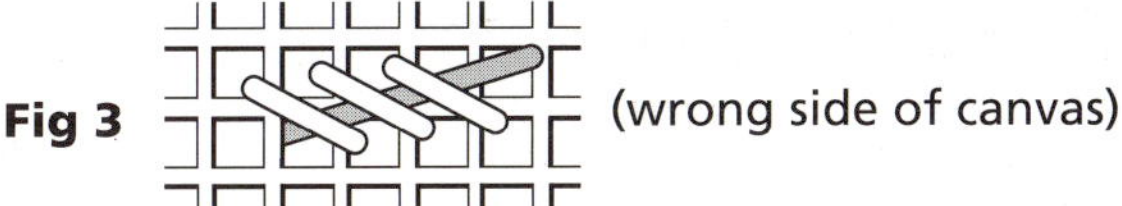

THE STITCHES

Continental Stitch

Most design areas are worked in Continental Stitch. This forms a flat diagonal stitch on the front of the canvas.

To work rows, bring the needle up through the canvas at odd numbers and down at even numbers (**Fig 4**). The rows can be worked from right to left or left to right; notice the difference in numbering, depending on the direction of the work.

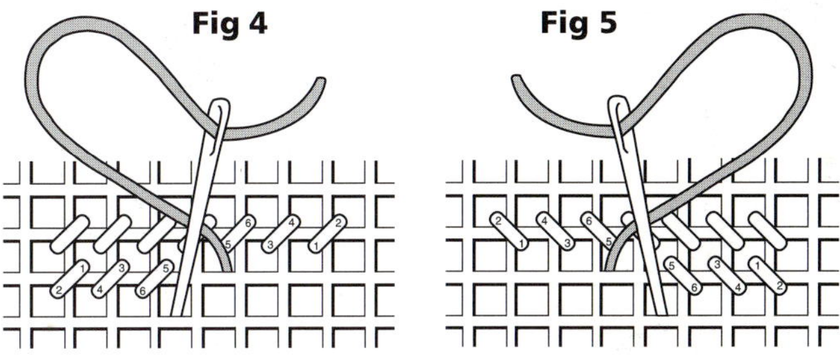

Occasionally a design requires a Reverse Continental Stitch where the stitches slope in the opposite direction. To work rows (**Fig 5**), bring needle up through canvas at odd numbers, down at even numbers.

Slanting Gobelin

Slanting Gobelin (pronounced like "go") is a long diagonal stitch that can be worked over any number of bars (**Fig 6**). Gobelin Stitches are indicated by long lines showing the exact placement of each stitch with color references in the color key.

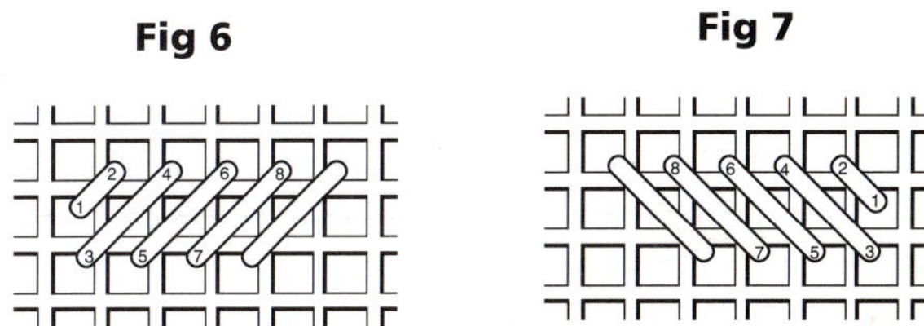

Reverse Slanting Gobelin Stitches slope in the opposite direction (**Fig 7**). Rows can be worked horizontally or vertically; direction will be shown on the chart.

Cross Stitch

Cross Stitch is used for decorative detail. It is worked over one or more bars; placement will be shown on the chart. Bring needle up at 1, down at 2, up at 3, and down at 4 to complete each stitch (**Fig 8**).

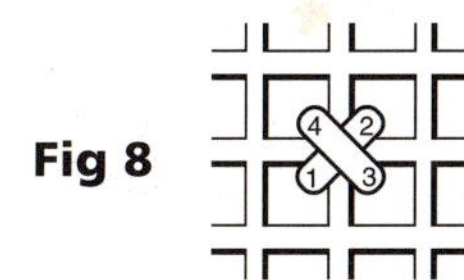

Straight Stitch

Straight Stitches can be made in any direction and over one or more bars; direction will be noted on the chart. They can be used for details and decorations worked on top of an area of completed stitching. Bring needle up at one end of the stitch and down at the other end (**Fig 9**).

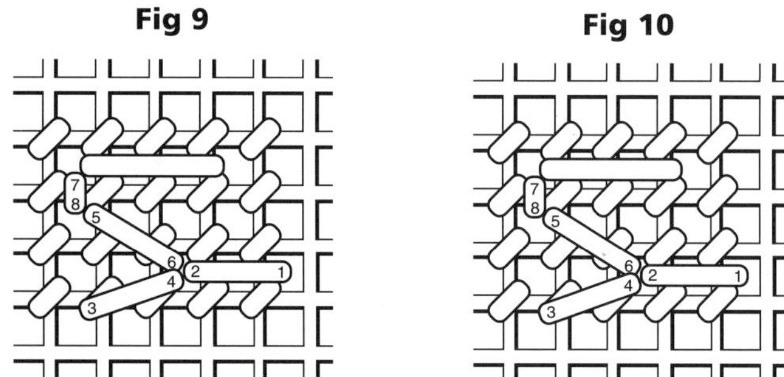

Fig 9   Fig 10

Straight Stitches can also be used to fill an area of canvas (**Fig 10**).

Backstitch

This is a straight stitch used for details and decoration, worked on top of an area of completed stitching (**Fig 11**). It is worked over one bar in any direction. The placement of the Backstitches will be indicated on the chart.

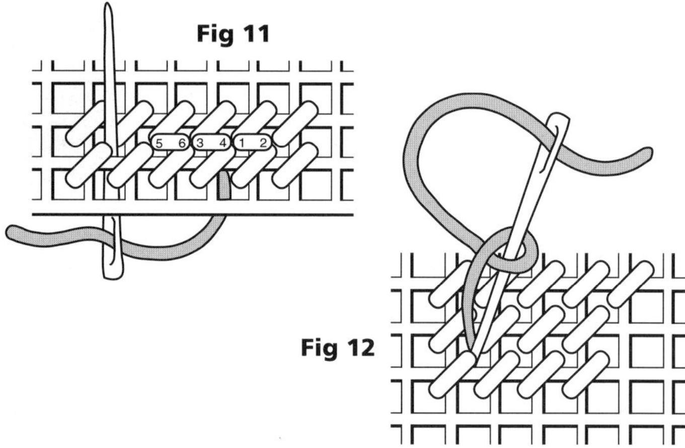

Fig 11

Fig 12

French Knot

The French Knot (**Fig 12**) is usually worked after the rest of the piece has been stitched. Bring needle up in center of hole, wrap strand around needle one time, and insert needle back down through same hole.

Mosaic Stitch

This is a square stitch worked over two bars (**Fig 13**), and can be worked in horizontal, vertical, or diagonal rows. The exact placement and direction of the stitches is indicated on the chart.

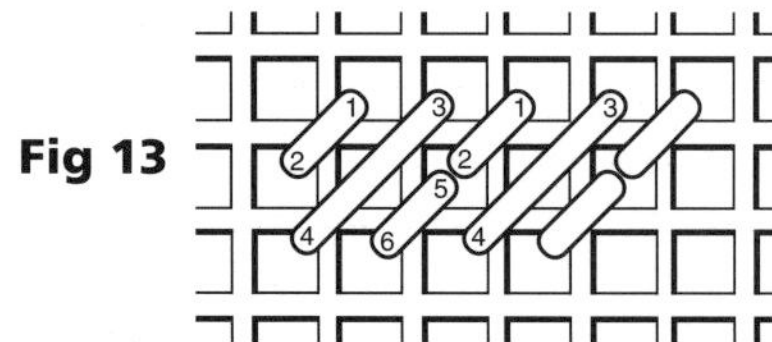

Fig 13

Kalem Stitch

The Kalem Stitch is a long stitch that is not worked on a perfect diagonal. The placement of the stitches is indicated on the chart. Follow the numbering in **Fig 14**, coming up at odd numbers and down at even numbers.

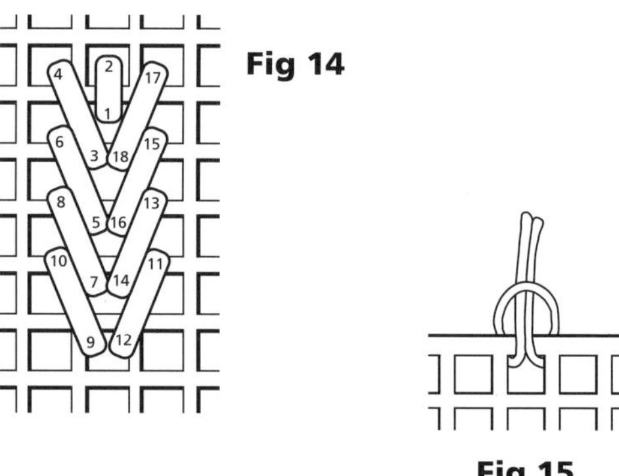

Fig 14

Fig 15

Fringe Knot

To make a Fringe Knot, thread both ends into needle. With canvas right side up, stitch up into a hole next to an outside bar, pass needle through resulting loop (**Fig 15**), then pull to tighten. Trim ends to the length specified in the project instructions.

Overcast Stitch

This stitch is used in two ways; to finish canvas edges or to join two pieces of canvas. Work from left to right or right to left, whichever is more comfortable.

To finish canvas edges, stitch loosely so strand will cover canvas (**Fig 16**). Take one stitch in each hole along a straight edge or into an inside corner, and three stitches when going around an outside corner. If the strand does not cover well, take additional stitches in each hole as needed.

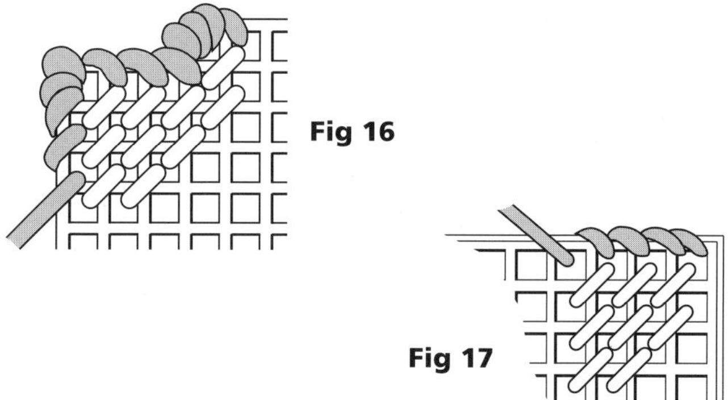

Fig 16

Fig 17

To join two pieces, hold pieces together and line up matching holes. Start joining with a holding stitch through the first hole of the two pieces, then continue joining (**Fig 17**), going through both pieces with each stitch. When ending off strand, tie a knot or weave end in securely.

On a curved or angled seam where holes will not match on the two pieces, it will be necessary to take additional stitches to compensate and cover the plastic edge.

THIS SNOWMAN'S A KEEPER

...FOR CARDS OR CANDY

MATERIALS

one sheet extra stiff 7-mesh plastic canvas
white embroidery floss
three red buttons, ½" diameter
three red beads, 4mm diameter
two holly charms, 19mm x 10½mm
monofilament line and sewing needle
three yds silver metallic yarn

worsted weight yarn:

white	63 yds
red	8 yds
orange	1 yd
gold	2 yds
green	3 yds
brown	2 yds
grey	3 yds
black	5 yds

INSTRUCTIONS

Step 1: From chart on page 4, draw outline and cut out Front. Following instructions in box below, draw outlines and cut out two Sides, Back, and Base.

Step 2: Stitch following chart. Work white floss Backstitches and orange Straight Stitches last, over previous stitching. Work Fringe Knots with 1" ends. Using red yarn, sew buttons to Front where indicated on chart. Using monofilament line and sewing needle, sew beads and holly leaves to Front at band of hat using cover photo as a guide.

Step 3: Refer to **Construction Diagram** for assembly. Using white, join side edges of Back to back edges of Sides, then overcast top edges of Back and Sides. Join front edges of Sides to wrong side of Front using white at left side; then white and grey to match previous stitching at right side. Using white, join Base to bottom edges of Back, Sides, and corresponding edge of Front.

Overcast remaining edges of Front using colors to match previous stitching.

Construction Diagram
(view from rear)

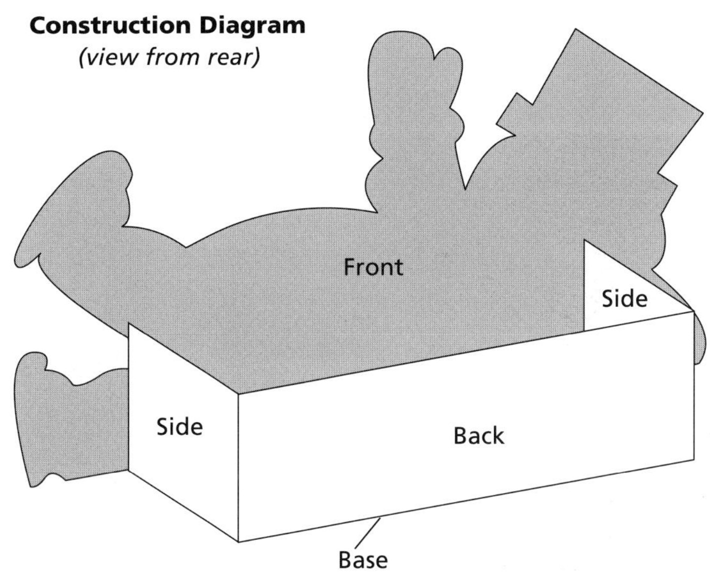

The following pieces are not charted. Cut and stitch as directed.

Side: This piece is cut 24 bars wide x 24 high. Cut two and fill in with white Slanting Gobelin worked in vertical columns over two bars.

Back: This piece is cut 52 bars wide x 24 high and is filled in with white Slanting Gobelin worked in vertical columns over two bars.

Base: This piece is cut 52 bars wide x 24 high and is left unstitched.

continued

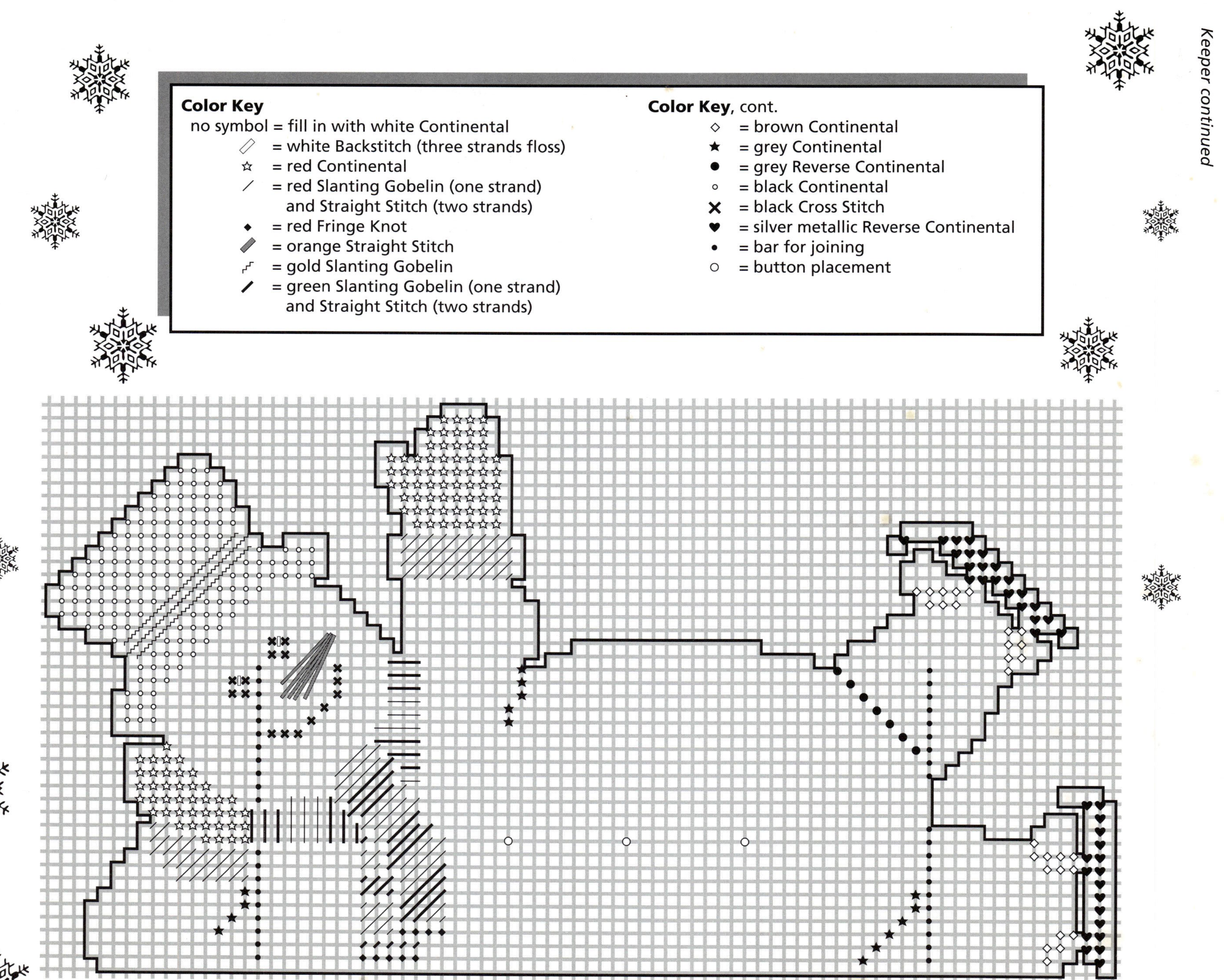

Color Key

no symbol = fill in with white Continental
▱ = white Backstitch (three strands floss)
☆ = red Continental
／ = red Slanting Gobelin (one strand)
and Straight Stitch (two strands)
◆ = red Fringe Knot
▨ = orange Straight Stitch
⌐ = gold Slanting Gobelin
╱ = green Slanting Gobelin (one strand)
and Straight Stitch (two strands)

Color Key, cont.
◇ = brown Continental
★ = grey Continental
● = grey Reverse Continental
○ = black Continental
✕ = black Cross Stitch
♥ = silver metallic Reverse Continental
• = bar for joining
○ = button placement

Front 82 bars wide x 44 high

FREEZE FRAME
...WITH 2½" x 4⅜" OPENING

MATERIALS
1½ sheets 7-mesh plastic canvas
white embroidery floss

worsted weight yarn:

white	21 yds
pink	1 yd
red	8 yds
orange	1 yd
med blue	4 yds
dk blue	4 yds
grey	3 yds
black	1 yd

INSTRUCTIONS

Step 1: Draw outlines and cut out Front, Back, and three Stands.

Step 2: Stitch Front following chart. Work white floss Backstitches and orange Straight Stitches last, over previous stitching. Work Fringe Knots on lower scarf edge with ¾" ends. Do not work Fringe Knots on upper scarf edge at this time. Overcast edges of cut out area of Front using white.

Step 3: Refer to **Construction Diagram** for assembly. Place all three Stands together and join top, bottom, and curved side edges using white. Join straight side edges of Stands to Back at bars indicated on chart. Place Back to wrong side of Front, matching side and bottom edges. Join matching edges of Front to Back using white; then work Fringe Knots with ¾" ends on upper scarf edge through both layers. Overcast remaining edges of Front using colors to match previous stitching.

Construction Diagram
(view from rear)

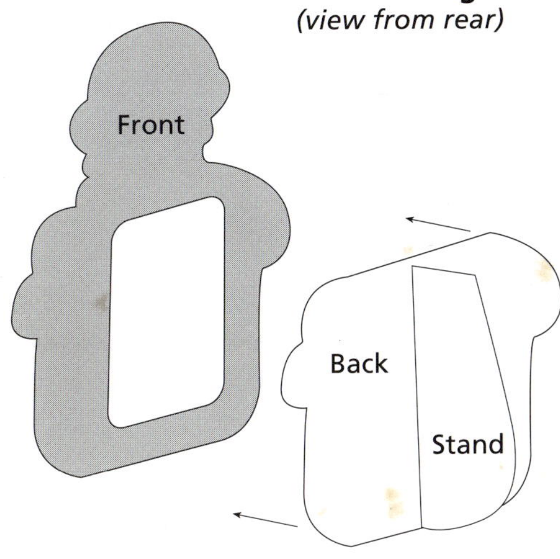

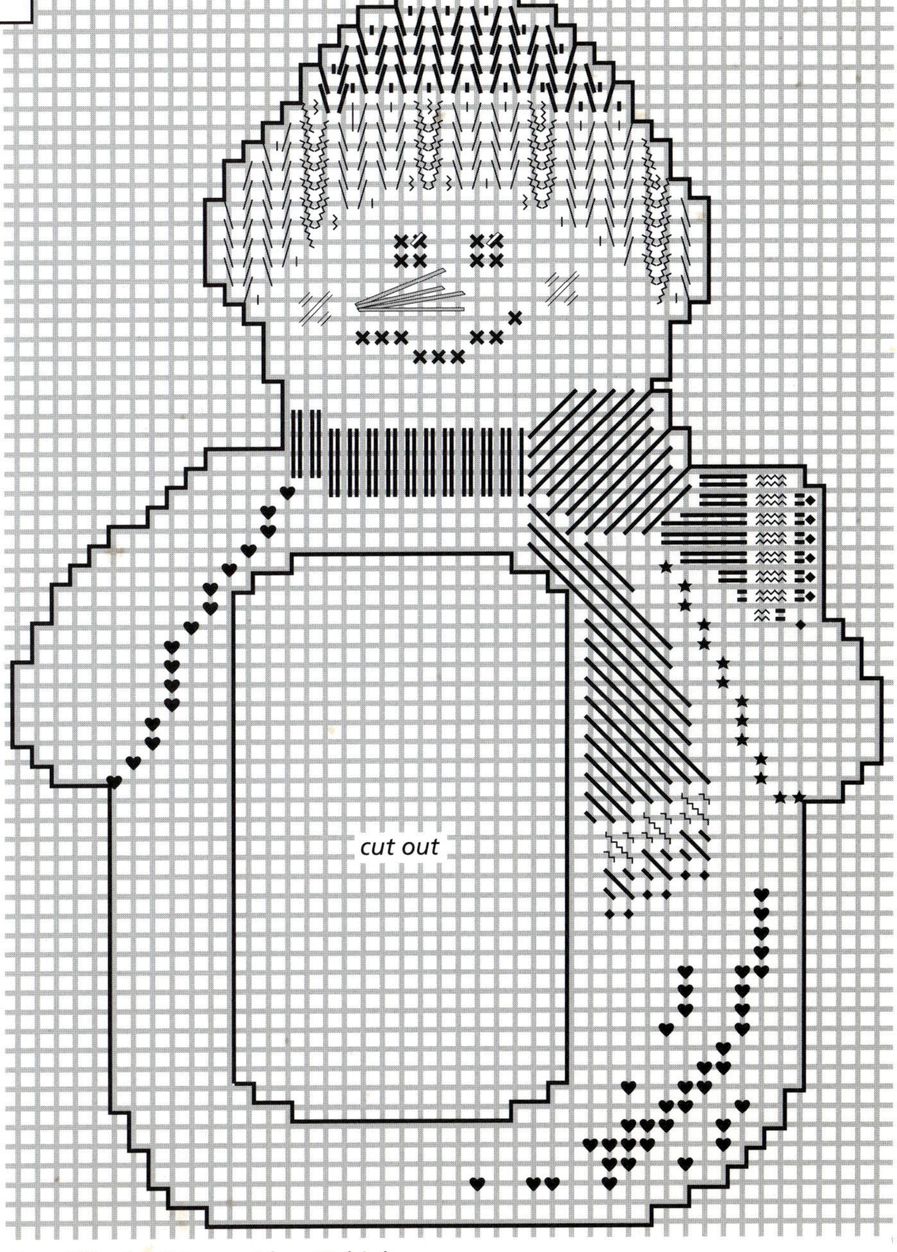

Front/Back 46 bars wide x 65 high

Color Key
no symbol = fill in with white Continental
⁄ = white Backstitch (four strands floss)
⫽ = pink Mosaic
⁄ = red Kalem, Slanting Gobelin, and Reverse Slanting Gobelin (one strand); and Straight Stitch (two strands)
⫽ = orange Straight Stitch
⁄ = med blue Kalem
⤴ = dk blue Mosaic, Kalem, and Straight Stitch
◆ = dk blue Fringe Knot
♥ = grey Continental
★ = grey Reverse Continental
✕ = black Cross Stitch

continued

Key
• = bar for joining

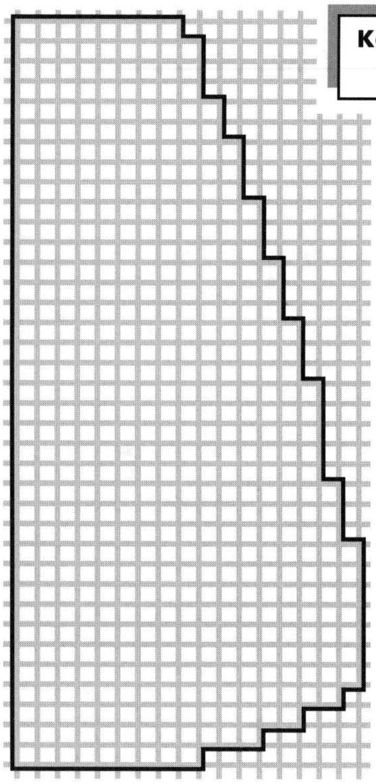

Stand 18 bars wide x 38 high
(cut 3 and leave unstitched)

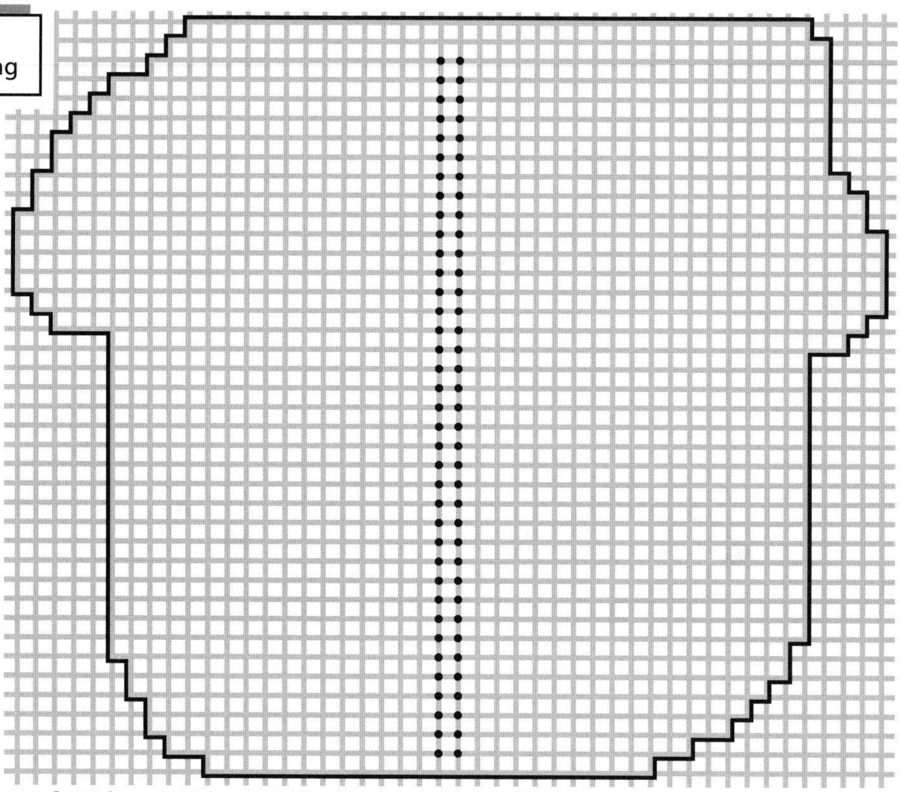

Back 46 bars wide x 40 high (leave unstitched)

SNOWED-IN DOORHANGER

MATERIALS
one sheet extra stiff 7-mesh plastic canvas
white embroidery floss
two dk yellow buttons, 3/8" diameter
six gold beads, 3mm diameter
3/4 yd gold wire, 20 gauge
monofilament line and sewing needle
six yds iridescent metallic yarn

worsted weight yarn:

white	12 yds
pink	1 yd
red	5 yds
orange	1 yd
dk yellow	3 yds
med blue	12 yds
dk blue	2 yds
black	8 yds

INSTRUCTIONS

Step 1: Draw outlines and cut out Snowman and three Flakes.

Step 2: Stitch following charts. Work white floss Backstitches and orange Straight Stitches last, over previous stitching. Work Fringe Knots with 3/4" ends. Overcast edges of Snowman using colors to match previous stitching. Overcast edges of Flakes using iridescent metallic yarn.

Sew buttons to Front for jacket using dk yellow yarn. Sew beads to Front for boots using monofilament line and sewing needle.

Step 3: Use cover photo as a guide to assemble hanger. Insert wire into Front at one mitten and twist a short length back around itself. Wrap wire around a pencil a few times, thread on one Flake, wrap wire around pencil several times, and thread on remaining Flakes in same manner. Insert remaining end of wire into other mitten and wrap around itself to secure.

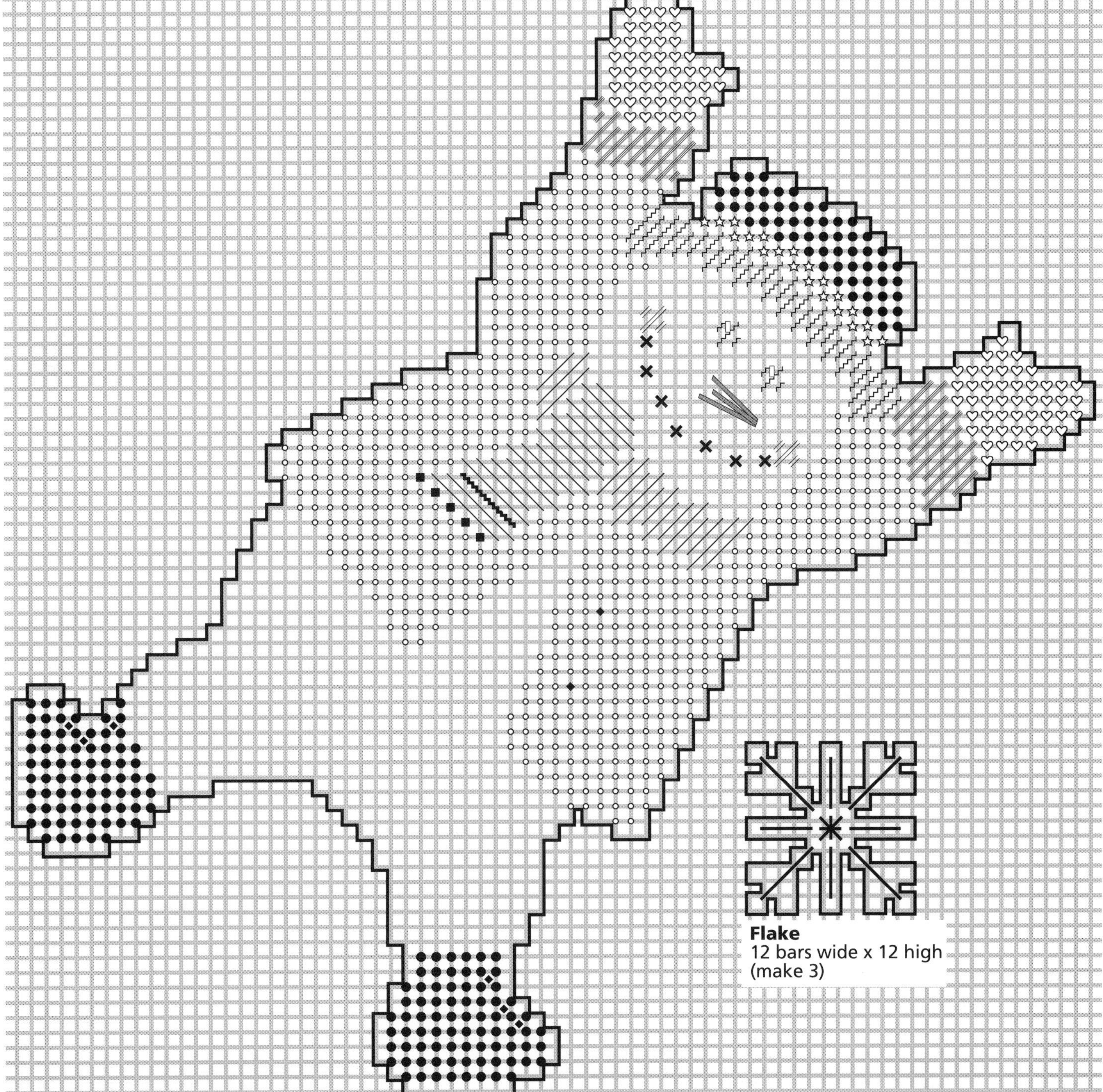

Flake
12 bars wide x 12 high
(make 3)

Snowman 73 bars wide x 74 high

SNOW FRIEND TISSUE BOX COVER
...FOR BOUTIQUE-SIZE TISSUE BOX

MATERIALS

two sheets 7-mesh plastic canvas

worsted weight yarn:

white	34 yds
pink	3 yds
med red	1 yd
dk red	8 yds
gold	11 yds
med blue	51 yds
dk blue	10 yds
black	3 yds

INSTRUCTIONS

Step 1: Draw outlines and cut out Front and three Sides.

Step 2: Stitch following charts. Work white Backstitches last, over previous stitching. Do not work Fringe Knots at this time.

Step 3: Join side edges of Sides and Front using colors to match previous stitching. When joining front edge of Side to scarf area of Front, join Side to bars for joining indicated on Front chart. Overcast resulting hole in top using med blue. Overcast remaining edges of Front and Sides using med blue and gold to match previous stitching. Work Fringe Knots with 1" ends.

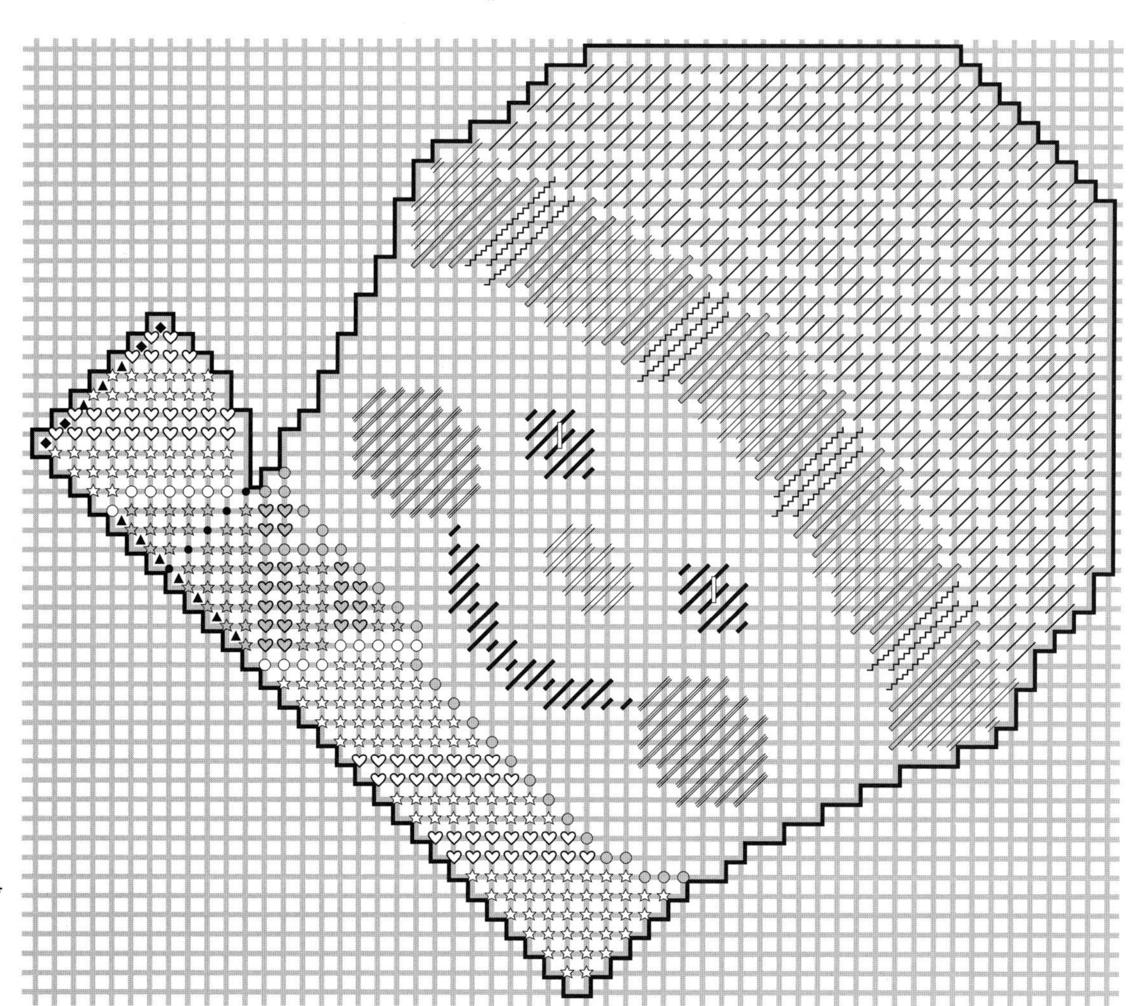

Front 57 bars wide x 50 high

Color Key

no symbol	=	fill in with white Continental
	=	white Backstitch
	=	pink Slanting Gobelin
	=	med red Slanting Gobelin
	=	dk red Slanting Gobelin
♡	=	gold Continental
♡	=	gold Reverse Continental
	=	gold Slanting Gobelin
◆	=	gold Fringe Knot
☆	=	med blue Continental
☆	=	med blue Reverse Continental
/	=	med blue Slanting Gobelin
▲	=	med blue Fringe Knot
○	=	dk blue Continental
●	=	dk blue Reverse Continental
	=	dk blue Slanting Gobelin
/	=	black Slanting Gobelin
•	=	bar for joining

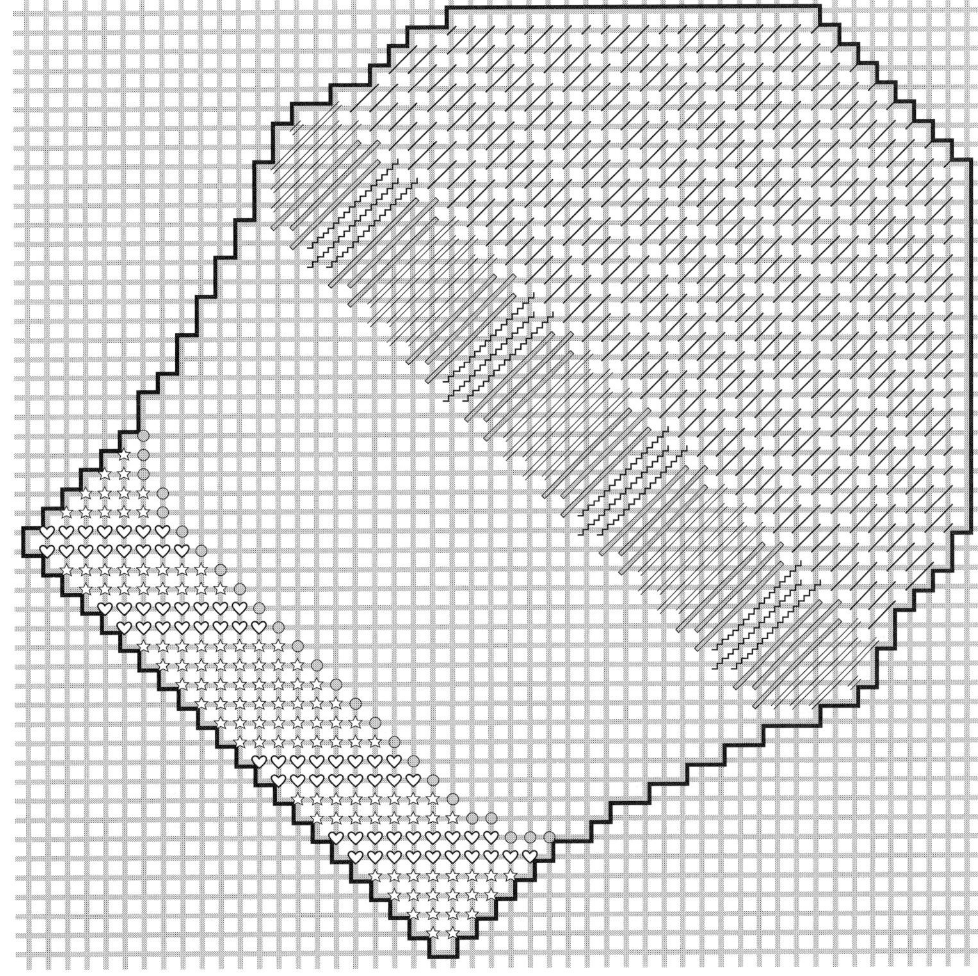

Side 50 bars wide x 50 high (make 3)

HAPPY SNOWMEN TREE ORNAMENTS
... INCLUDING BIRD MAN, BROOM MAN, AND TREE MAN

MATERIALS *(for all three ornaments)*
1½ sheets 7-mesh plastic canvas
black embroidery floss
three yds natural raffia
three red beads, 4mm diameter
seven black cabochons, 4mm diameter
monofilament line and sewing needle
one yd gold thread
gold jump ring, 6mm diameter
tacky craft glue or hot glue

worsted weight yarn:

white	30 yds	med blue	3 yds
pink	2 yds	dk blue	2 yds
med red	3 yds	rust	3 yds
dk red	4 yds	med brown	1 yd
med yellow	1 yd	dk brown	3 yds
dk yellow	4 yds	grey	1 yd
med green	4 yds	black	5 yds
dk green	3 yds		

Color Key (for Bird Man)
no symbol = fill in with white Continental
╱╱ = pink Mosaic
○ = med red Continental
◉ = med red Reverse Continental
● = dk red Continental
╱ = dk red Straight Stitch
◇ = dk yellow Continental
♡ = med green Continental
♥ = med green Reverse Continental
• = med green Fringe Knot
☆ = dk blue Continental
╱ = dk blue Straight Stitch
★ = rust Reverse Continental
△ = black Continental
▲ = black Reverse Continental
⌐ = black Straight Stitch (six strands floss)
◆ = bead and cabochon placement

INSTRUCTIONS

Step 1: Draw outlines and cut out Bird Man, Birdhouse, Broom, Broom Man, Tree Man, Tree, Scarf, two Left Arms, and two Right Arms.

Step 2: Stitch following charts. Work black floss Straight Stitches last, over previous stitching. Do not work med red Backstitches on Broom at this time. Work Fringe Knots with ¾" ends. Overcast bird beak on Bird Man using med yellow. Overcast edge of Tree Man's head between earmuffs using grey. Overcast remaining edges of all pieces using colors to match previous stitching. Work med red Backstitches on Broom, piercing the raffia where necessary.

Step 3: Using monofilament line and sewing needle, sew beads to Men for noses where indicated on charts. Glue cabochons to Men for eyes where indicated on charts.

Step 4: Use cover photo as a guide to assembly. Use jump ring to attach top of Birdhouse to Bird Man. Glue one set of Arms holding Broom to Broom Man. Glue other set of Arms holding Tree to Tree Man; then glue Scarf behind Tree Man's left shoulder. Cut gold metallic thread into three equal lengths and thread each length through top of each snowman for hangers.

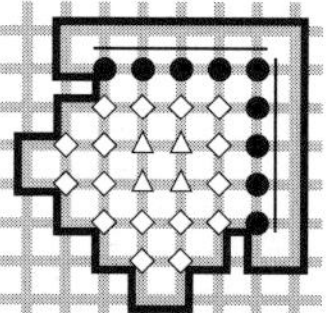

Birdhouse
8 bars wide x 8 high

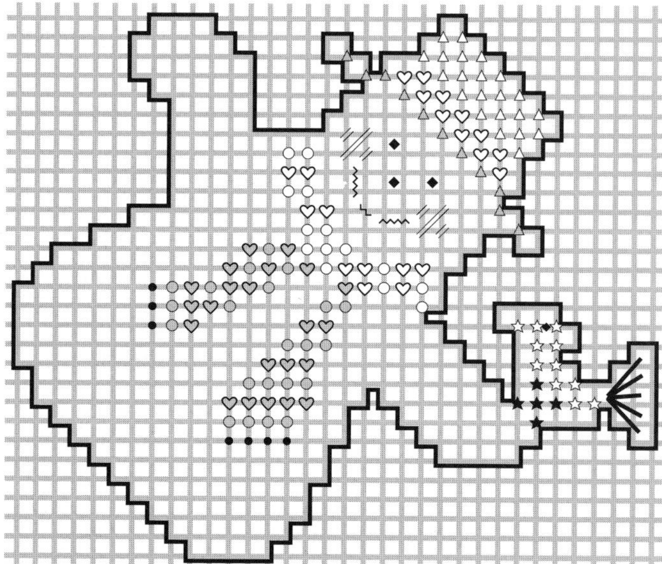

Bird Man 34 bars wide x 29 high

Color Key (for Broom Man, Broom, and Arms)

no symbol = fill in with white Continental
- ⁄⁄ = pink Mosaic
- ♡ = med red Continental
- ♥ = med red Reverse Continental
- ╱ = med red Backstitch
- ☆ = med blue Continental
- ★ = med blue Reverse Continental
- ◆ = med blue Fringe Knot
- ● = dk brown Continental
- ○ = black Continental
- ⌐ = black Slanting Gobelin
- ╱ = black Straight Stitch (six strands floss)
- ⁄⁄ = raffia Slanting Gobelin
- • = bead and cabochon placement

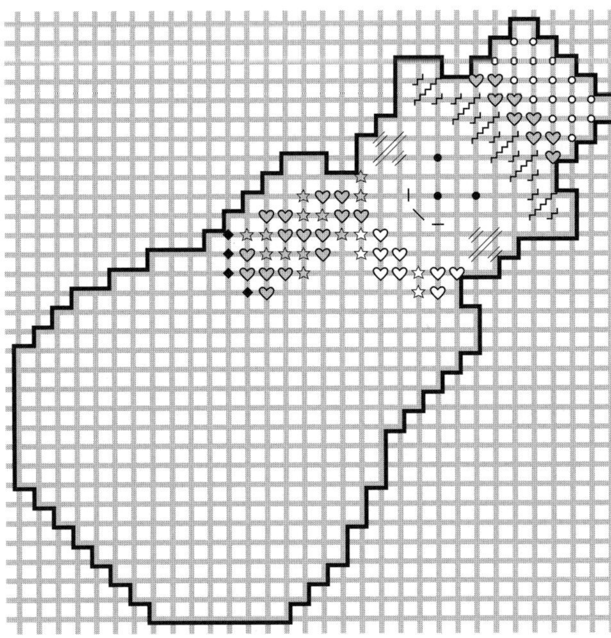

Broom Man 32 bars wide x 32 high

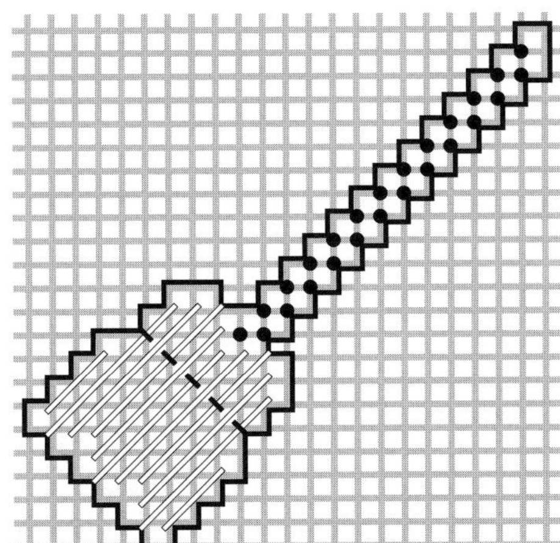

Broom 23 bars wide x 23 high

Color Key (for Tree Man, Tree, and Scarf)

no symbol = fill in with white Continental
- ⁄⁄ = pink Mosaic
- ⌐ = dk red Slanting Gobelin and Reverse Slannting Gobelin
- ◆ = dk red Fringe Knot
- ╱ = dk yellow Slanting Gobelin and Reverse Slanting Gobelin
- ⁄⁄ = dk green Slanting Gobelin
- ⁄⁄ = med brown Straight Stitch
- ☆ = grey Continental
- ╱ = black Straight Stitch (six strands floss)
- • = bead and cab0chon placement

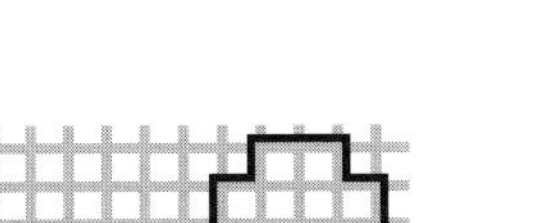

Left Arm
11 bars wide x 11 high
(make 2)

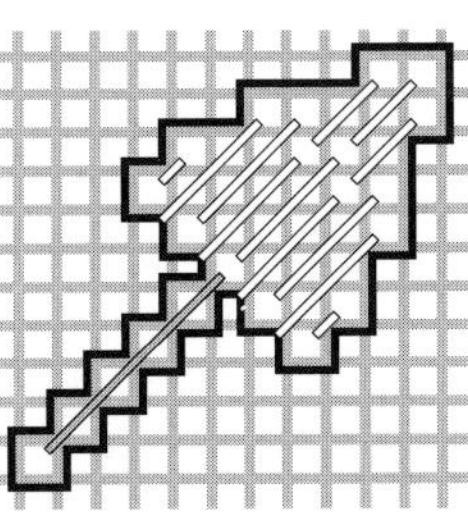

Tree
12 bars wide x 12 high

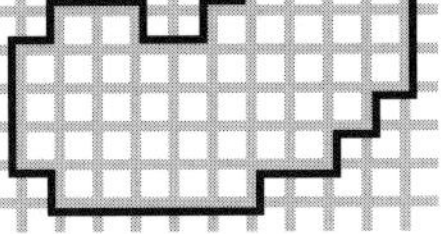

Right Arm
10 bars wide x 11 high
(make 2)

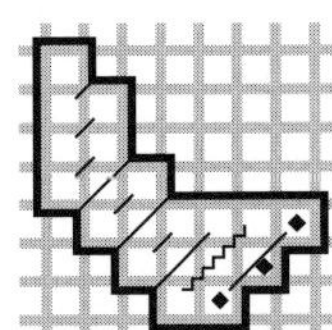

Scarf
8 bars wide x 8 high

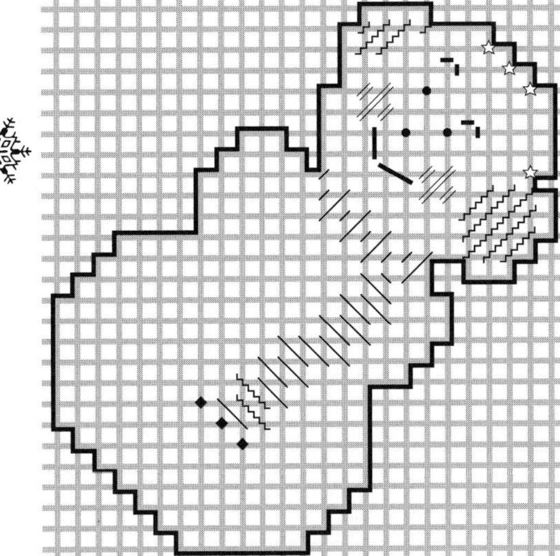

Tree Man 25 bars wide x 27 high

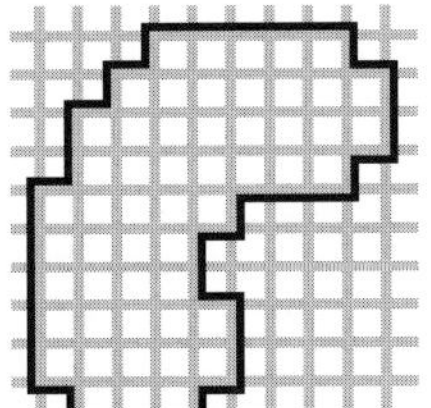

LOVING COUPLE
...WITH NUMERALS FOR ANY YEAR

MATERIALS

½ sheet 7-mesh plastic canvas
two yds white #3 pearl cotton
embroidery floss (white and grey)
two red beads, 4mm diameter
four black cabochons, 4mm diameter
monofilament line and sewing needle
8" length gold metallic thread
tacky craft glue or hot glue

worsted weight yarn:

white	9 yds
lt pink	1 yd
med pink	3 yds
dk pink	2 yds
dk red	4 yds
gold	3 yds
blue	3 yds
black	3 yds

INSTRUCTIONS

Step 1: Draw outlines and cut out Couple and Heart.

Step 2: Stitch following charts. Work Backstitches and Straight Stitches last, over previous stitching. Work desired numbers on Heart. Work Fringe Knots with ³/₄" ends. Overcast edges of Couple and Heart using colors to match previous stitching.

Step 3: Using monofilament line and sewing needle, sew beads to Couple for noses where indicated on chart. Glue cabochons to Couple for eyes where indicated on chart. Using white, tack top of Heart arms to shoulders of Couple; Heart will bow outward. Thread gold metallic thread through tops of hats for hanger.

Color Key

no symbol	= fill in with white Continental
╱	= white Straight Stitch (pearl cotton)
×	= lt pink Cross Stitch
◇	= med pink Continental
◈	= med pink Reverse Continental
•	= med pink Fringe Knot
○	= dk pink Continental
◉	= dk pink Reverse Continental
▱	= dk pink Slanting Gobelin
○	= dk red Continental
☆	= gold Continental
★	= gold Reverse Continental
⌐	= gold Slanting Gobelin and Reverse Slanting Gobelin
▲	= gold Fringe Knot
♡	= blue Continental
╱	= grey Backstitch (six strands floss)
♥	= black Continental
⫽	= black Slanting Gobelin
⫽	= black Straight Stitch (six strands floss)
◆	= bead and cabochon placement

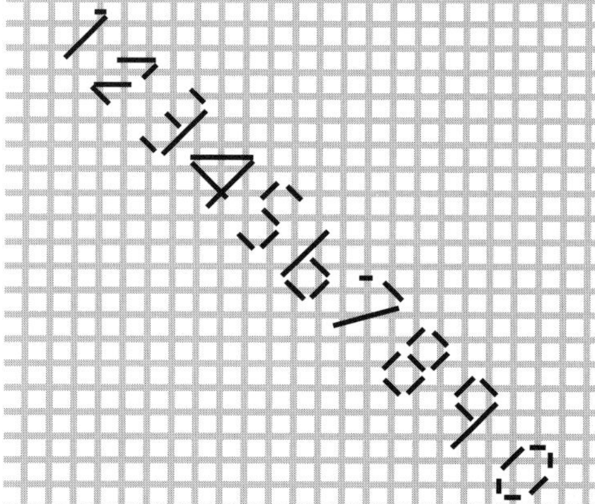

Numbers

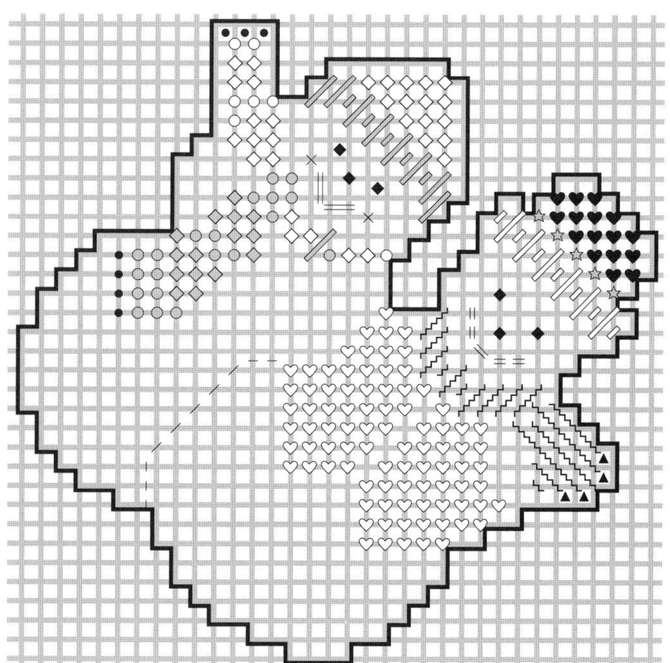

Couple 34 bars wide x 34 high

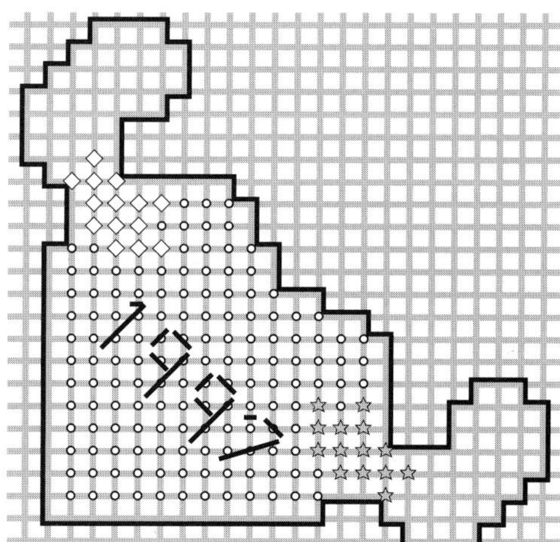

Heart 24 bars wide x 24 high

WINTER WONDERLAND COASTERS
...WITH A FOREST OF PINE TREES HOLDER

MATERIALS *(for holder and four coasters)*
3¹/₂ sheets 7-mesh plastic canvas
white embroidery floss
three 5" lengths wooden dowel, ¹/₄" diameter

worsted wieght yarn:

white	48 yds	med blue	4 yds
pink	2 yds	dk blue	4 yds
med red	5 yds	lt purple	4 yds
dk red	4 yds	med purple	4 yds
gold	3 yds	lt rust	4 yds
lt green	3 yds	med rust	4 yds
med green	3 yds	brown	8 yds
dk green	53 yds	black	10 yds
lt blue	3 yds		

INSTRUCTIONS

Step 1: Draw outlines and cut out three Bases, six Trees, and four Coasters.

Step 2: Stitch following charts. For Base, hold all three together and stitch through all as if they were one. For Coasters, work vest, hat band, and mittens as follows.

Coaster A: lt vest color med red, dk vest color dk red, hat band and mitten color med green

Coaster B: lt vest color lt purple, dk vest color med purple, hat band and mitten color lt blue

Coaster C: lt vest color med blue, dk vest color dk blue, hat band and mitten color gold

Coaster D: lt vest color lt rust, dk vest color med rust, hat band and mitten color lt green

Work Backstitches and Straight Stitches last, over previous stitching. Overcast edges of Base and Coasters using colors to match previous stitching. Overcast trunk edges of Trees using brown.

Step 3: Place two Trees with wrong sides together and one dowel length sandwiched in between; then join remaining edges using dk green. Repeat for remaining Trees and dowels. Spread trunks of one Tree and join to Base at one set of bars for joining indicated on chart using brown. Join remaining Trees to Base in same manner.

Color Key (for Base)
no symbol = fill in with white Continental
/ = white Slanting Gobelin
• = bar for joining

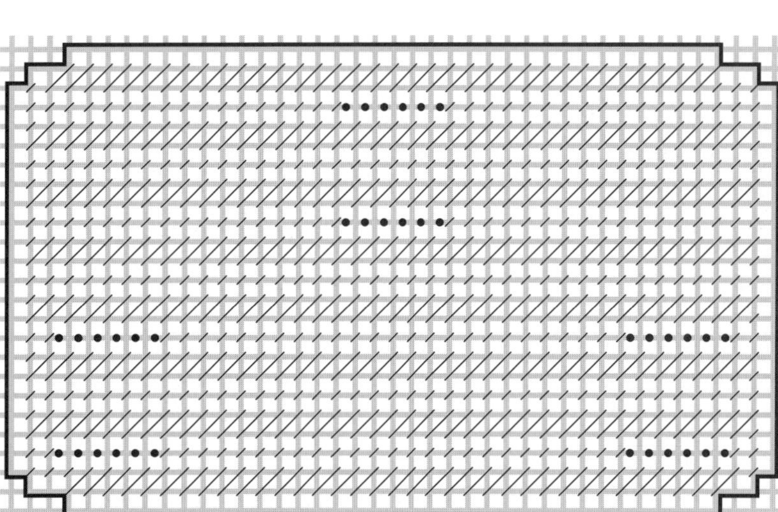

Base 41 bars wide x 25 high
(cut 3; hold together as one and stitch through all)

continued

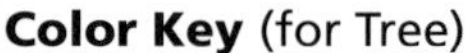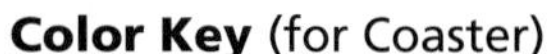

Color Key (for Tree)
/ = dk green Slanting Gobelin
/ = brown Slanting Gobelin

Color Key (for Coaster)
no symbol = fill in with white Continental
/ = white Back Stitch (six strands floss)
// = lt pink Mosaic
× = med red Cross Stitch
/ = med red Backstitch
• = black Continental
✕ = black Cross Stitch
/ = black Slanting Gobelin and Straight Stitch
○ = lt vest Continental (see Step 2)
★ = dk vest Continental (see Step 2)
● = mitten Continental (see Step 2)
⌐ = hat Slanting Gobelin (see Step 2)

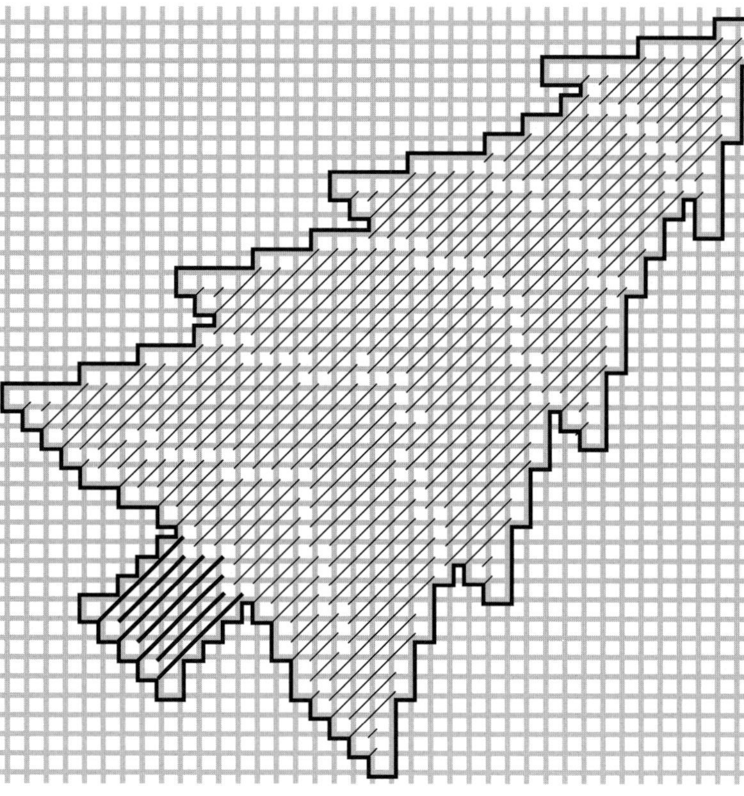

Tree 40 bars wide x 40 high (make 6)

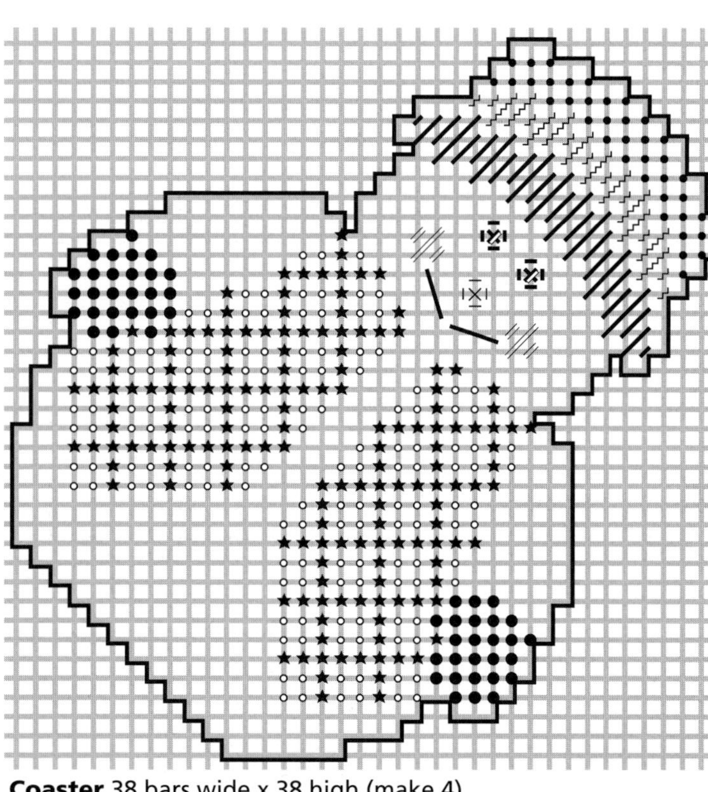

Coaster 38 bars wide x 38 high (make 4)

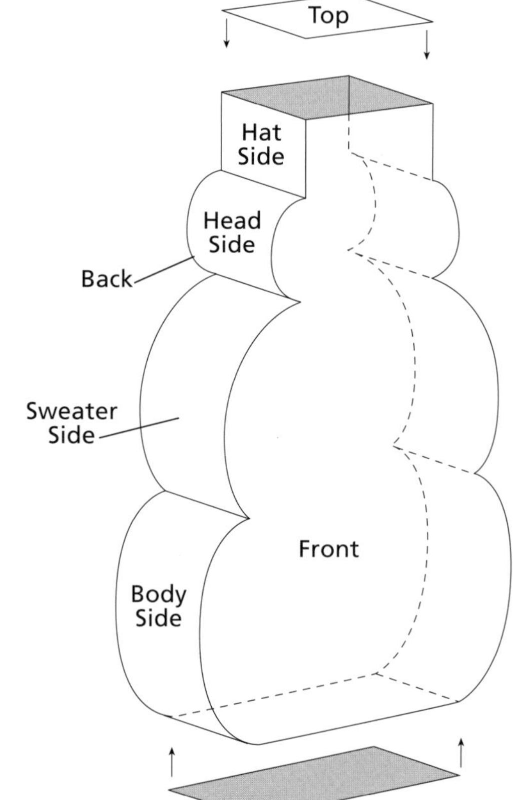

Dandy Doorstop
Construction Diagram

DANDY DOORSTOP
...IN DESIGNER SWEATER

MATERIALS

1½ sheets extra stiff 7-mesh plastic canvas
one sheet extra soft 7-mesh plastic canvas
embroidery floss (white and blue)
six yds natural raffia
desired weight (see **Note** below)
tacky craft glue or hot glue

worsted weight yarn:

white	81 yds	med orange	3 yds
pink	2 yds	gold	3 yds
med red	17 yds	green	85 yds
dk red	1 yd	brown	4 yds
lt orange	1 yd	black	38 yds

Note: Use a standard size (8" x 4" x 2") brick for weight. Cover the brick with plastic wrap to keep doorstop clean. Other materials, such as sand, gravel, dried beans, or rice can be placed in a plastic sealable bag and used as a weight.

INSTRUCTIONS

Step 1: From stiff canvas, draw outlines and cut out Left Bird, Right Bird, Left Wing, Right Wing, two Hat Brims, Broom, Nose Side A, Nose Side B, Lower Nose, two Front/Back, Top, and Base.

From soft canvas, draw outlines and cut out two Hat Sides, two Sweater Sides, two Body Sides, Left Arm, Right Arm, and two Head Sides.

Step 2: Stitch following charts. Note that Back is stitched with white Continental for entire head area. Work white floss Backstitches and blue floss French Knots last, over previous stitching. Do not work med red Backstitches on Broom at this time. Overcast edges of Broom using raffia and brown to match previous stitches; then work med red Backstitches, piercing raffia where necessary. Overcast edges of Arms using med red and green to match previous stitching. Place Hat Brims with wrong sides together and join all edges using black.

Step 3: Refer to **Construction Diagram** on page 14 for assembly. Make a strip as follows: join bottom edge of one Hat Side to top edge of one Head Side using white; join bottom edge of Head Side to top edge of one Sweater Side using white; and join bottom edge of Sweater Side to top edge of one Body Side using green. Repeat for remaining Side pieces.

Join front edges of two strips to side edges of Front using colors to match previous stitching. Using green, tack Arms to Sweater Sides at shoulders, using cover photo as a guide. Join Back to back edges of strips in same manner. Using black, join Top to top edges of Front, Back, and Hat Sides. Place desired weight up into snowman. Join bottom edges of Front, Back, and Body Sides to Base using white.

Overcast edges of Wings using med red. Place Left Bird and Right Bird with wrong sides together; join edges using lt orange for beak, black for face, and med red for remaining edges.

Using med orange, join bottom edges of Nose Side A and Nose Side B to side edges of Lower Nose; then overcast remaining edges.

Step 4: Glue Wings to Bird. Glue Nose to Front at face. Place Hat Brim over top. Glue Bird to Hat Brim. Glue Broom to Arms, using cover photo as a guide.

The following pieces are not charted. Cut and stitch as directed.
Top: This piece is cut 18 bars wide x 18 high from stiff canvas and is filled in with black Continental.
Base: This piece is cut 28 bars wide x 18 high from stiff canvas and is left unstitched.
Head Side: This piece is cut 18 bars wide x 20 high. Cut two from soft canvas and fill in with white Continental.

Color Key
no symbol = fill in with med red Continental
  / = med red Straight Stitch (two strands)
  / = Wing Straight Stitch (one strand med red and one strand dk red)
  ◆ = blue French Knot (six strands floss)
  ○ = black Continental

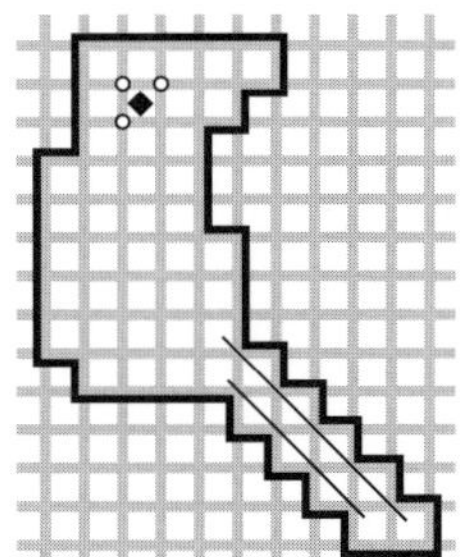

Left Bird
11 bars wide x 14 high
(stiff canvas)

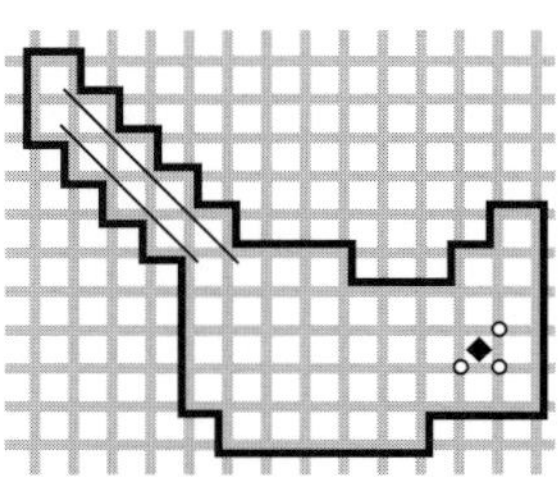

Right Bird
14 bars wide x 11 high
(stiff canvas)

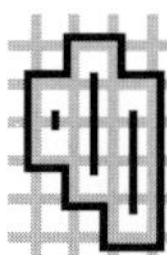

Left Wing
4 bars wide x 6 high
(stiff canvas)

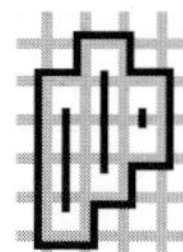

Right Wing
4 bars wide x 6 high
(stiff canvas)

continued

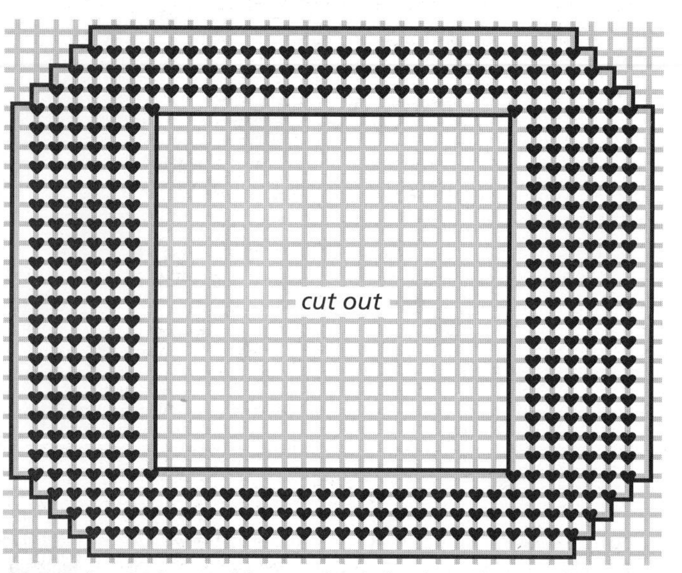

Hat Brim 34 bars wide x 28 high (make 2 from stiff canvas)

Lower Nose
4 bars wide x 9 high
(stiff canvas)

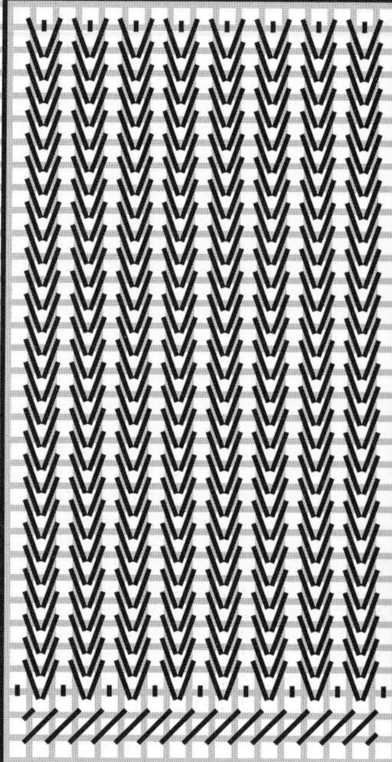

Sweater Side
18 bars wide x 34 high
(cut 2 from soft canvas)

Hat Side
18 bars wide x 13 high
(cut 2 from stiff canvas)

Color Key

no symbol = fill in with white Continental
/ = white Slanting Gobelin
⟋ = white Backstitch (six strands floss)
⫽ = pink Slanting Gobelin
♡ = med red Continental
♥ = med red Reverse Continental
⌐ = med red Kalem, Slanting Gobelin,
     Reverse Slanting Gobelin, and Backstitch
○ = med orange Continental
● = med orange Reverse Continental
⫽ = gold Kalem
/ = green Kalem and Slanting Gobelin
★ = brown Continental
• = black Continental
✕ = black Cross Stitch
⫽ = raffia Slanting Gobelin

Nose Side A
9 bars wide x 4 high
(stiff canvas)

Nose Side B
9 bars wide x 4 high
(stiff canvas)

Body Side 18 bars wide x 37 high
(make 2 from soft canvas)

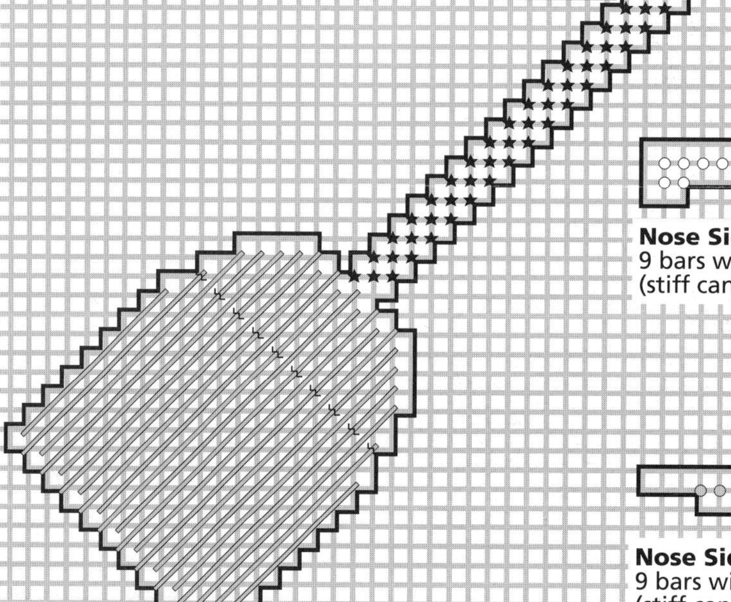

Broom 50 bars wide x 50 high (stiff canvas)